"Whispers of Possibility"

Chapter 1: The Chance Encounter

Chapter 2: A Twist of Fate

Chapter 3: The Hidden Fortune

Chapter 4: Love in the Shadows

Chapter 5: Unveiling the Dark Underworld

Chapter 6: The Streets Ignite

Chapter 1: The Chance Encounter

As the sun dipped below the horizon, casting a warm orange glow over the bustling city streets, fate began to weave its intricate web. In the heart of downtown, amidst the swirl of hurried footsteps and the symphony of car horns, two lives on divergent paths were about to converge.

Meet Sophia Reynolds, a vivacious and ambitious young woman who had always dreamt of a life filled with adventure and success. Her pursuit of a thriving career had taken her to the heart of the city, where she worked tirelessly as a financial analyst for a prestigious firm. Sophia's days were consumed by numbers and charts, leaving little room for anything else.

On this particular evening, Sophia found herself standing on a crowded street corner, her mind lost in a flurry of thoughts about deadlines and meetings. Oblivious to her surroundings, she accidentally collided with a stranger, causing both of them to stumble.

Apologies tumbled out of Sophia's mouth as her gaze met the piercing blue eyes of a man she had inadvertently bumped into. His name was Anthony Marino, a charismatic and enigmatic figure with a reputation that preceded him. Anthony had grown up in the gritty underbelly of the city, navigating a world rife with crime and danger. However, he had managed to rise through the ranks of the local mafia, becoming a formidable force to be reckoned with.

In that brief moment of collision, their lives intersected, and an inexplicable spark ignited between them. Sophia, captivated by Anthony's magnetic presence, felt an unfamiliar rush of excitement and curiosity. Anthony, on the other hand, saw in Sophia a glimmer of innocence and purity that had long been absent from his own tumultuous existence.

Drawn by an invisible force, they found themselves engaged in an unexpected conversation. Sophia, eager to escape the monotony of her everyday life, was intrigued by Anthony's tales of danger, power, and the allure of the forbidden. Anthony, in turn, was captivated by Sophia's intelligence, ambition, and the untapped potential he sensed within her.

As the night wore on, their encounter took an unexpected turn. Anthony, driven by a desire to protect Sophia from the sinister forces that lurked in the shadows, offered her an opportunity that would forever alter the course of her life. He proposed an audacious plan—a collaboration that would involve delving into the clandestine world of the mafia, using Sophia's financial acumen to navigate the treacherous waters of money laundering and illicit transactions.

Though hesitant at first, Sophia's thirst for adventure and her longing for something more than her mundane existence pushed her to take a leap of faith. She found herself entangled in a dangerous dance with the mafia, where every step she took carried both the promise of success and the threat of devastating consequences.

Little did Sophia know that her journey would not only test her courage and resilience but also plunge her into a whirlwind of love, betrayal, and relentless pursuit by the FBI. As the whispers of possibility beckoned, Sophia and Anthony embarked on an exhilarating and perilous ride that would challenge their notions of right and wrong, loyalty and betrayal, and ultimately, their own identities.

Chapter 1 ended with Sophia standing at the precipice of a life-altering decision, her heart torn between the allure of an extraordinary existence and the safety of the world she had always known. In the depths of her soul, she sensed that the choice she was about to make would have far-reaching consequences, forever changing the trajectory of her life.

Sophia stood at the precipice of a life-altering decision, her heart pounding in her chest as she weighed the risks and rewards that lay before her. Anthony's proposition had ignited a fire within her, stirring a dormant sense of adventure and a longing for a life outside the confines of her predictable existence.

Over the next few days, Sophia delved deeper into the world Anthony had introduced her to. She meticulously researched the inner workings of the mafia, becoming well-versed in their intricate web of power, money, and deceit. At the same time, she studied the tactics and strategies employed by the FBI to bring down criminal organizations, ensuring that she understood the game being played on both sides.

As their collaboration deepened, Sophia discovered a newfound sense of purpose and excitement. She reveled in the adrenaline rush that came from the risks they took and the intricate plans they devised. The allure of the forbidden and the intoxicating power she felt within the inner circle of the mafia consumed her thoughts.

However, as Sophia became more entangled in this dangerous world, cracks began to appear in her carefully constructed façade. She found herself torn between her loyalty to Anthony and the growing affection she felt for him, and the nagging voice of conscience that reminded her of the lives being destroyed by their actions.

Love, too, had entered the equation. Sophia met Alex, an idealistic and determined FBI agent, during one of her encounters with Anthony. Their paths crossed unexpectedly, and a connection sparked between them.

Alex, unaware of Sophia's involvement with the mafia, saw in her a kindred spirit—a desire for justice and a longing to make a difference. Their shared values and unwavering dedication to their respective causes created a powerful magnetism between them.

Sophia found herself torn between her blossoming feelings for Alex and the pull of the dangerous world she had willingly immersed herself in with Anthony. The lines between right and wrong blurred as she navigated a treacherous landscape where trust was a luxury and betrayal loomed at every turn.

Meanwhile, the FBI had begun closing in on the mafia, closing the net around the criminal organization that Anthony was a part of. Sophia's dual role as Anthony's confidante and a potential informant for the FBI put her in an increasingly precarious position. She had to tread carefully, ensuring her true alliances remained concealed as she collected information and played a dangerous game of deception.

With each passing day, the stakes grew higher, and the tension mounted. Sophia's loyalty to Anthony wavered as she witnessed the devastating consequences of the mafia's actions. Innocent lives were destroyed, families torn apart, and the dark underbelly of the city's criminal empire laid bare before her.

As the pressure intensified, Sophia found herself at a crossroads. The whispers of possibility that had once enticed her now whispered warnings. She had to confront her own morality, face the consequences of her choices, and decide where her true allegiance lay.

Chapter 1 closed with Sophia standing on the precipice of a life-altering decision. She knew that whatever path she chose would have far-reaching consequences, not only for herself but for those she cared about. In the depths of her soul, she grappled with the conflicting desires for love, justice, and the intoxicating allure of a life filled with power and danger.

Little did Sophia know that her journey was far from over. The path she had chosen would lead her down a treacherous road, testing her resilience, her loyalties, and her very sense of self. In the chapters that lay ahead, she would discover the true nature of love, the price of betrayal, and the lengths one must go to find redemption in a world consumed by darkness.

As the whispers of possibility echoed in her mind, Sophia took a deep breath and made her choice. Her destiny was intertwined with the fates of those around her, and she was about to embark on a journey that would challenge her in ways she could never have imagined.

Chapter 2: A Twist of Fate

Sophia's decision reverberated through her being as she stepped into the murky depths of her chosen path. The shadows of the city seemed to embrace her, whispering secrets and conspiracies as she ventured further into the heart of the mafia's operations.

Under Anthony's guidance, Sophia became a trusted confidante, her financial expertise proving invaluable in their illicit endeavors. She maneuvered through the intricacies of money laundering with a deftness that surprised even herself. The lines between legality and criminality blurred as she delved deeper into the world of dirty money, hidden transactions, and complex schemes.

As Sophia grew more entrenched in this treacherous realm, her relationship with Anthony evolved. What had initially been a business partnership tinged with intrigue transformed into something deeper—a connection forged amidst danger and shared secrets. Sophia found herself drawn to Anthony's enigmatic charisma, his ability to navigate the dark alleys of the city with both cunning and ruthlessness.

Yet, as their bond deepened, Sophia couldn't shake the nagging feeling that she was losing a part of herself in the process. The allure of power and the adrenaline rush of their exploits clouded her judgment, blinding her to the consequences of her actions. She was on a collision course with her own moral compass, and the collision was imminent.

Meanwhile, her chance encounter with Alex, the FBI agent, continued to haunt her thoughts. Their connection, though brief, had left an indelible mark on Sophia's heart. She couldn't help but wonder if there was a way out of this tangled web she had woven for herself—a way to reconcile her desire for justice with the dangerous path she had chosen.

One fateful evening, as Sophia and Anthony met with their mafia contacts in a dimly lit warehouse, a ripple of tension filled the air. Unbeknownst to them, the FBI had received a tip about the meeting and had orchestrated a carefully planned raid. Chaos erupted as armed agents stormed in, their guns drawn and voices commanding the surrender of everyone present.

Sophia's heart raced as panic and fear gripped her. In the midst of the chaos, she caught sight of Alex, his determined gaze filled with a mix of surprise and concern. Their eyes locked for a brief moment, and Sophia's heart sank—her secret life was on the verge of being exposed, and the consequences would be dire.

In a desperate bid to protect herself and Anthony, Sophia's survival instincts kicked in. She broke free from the grip of the chaos, her mind racing to find an escape route. With her heart pounding and adrenaline fueling her every move, she darted through the labyrinthine corridors of the warehouse, evading both the FBI and the enraged mafia members who sought to capture her.

As she ran, a myriad of emotions surged within her—fear, regret, and the lingering hope that somehow, she could find a way to extricate herself from the clutches of this dangerous world. Her thoughts turned to Alex, wondering if he understood the complexities of her situation or if he saw her merely as a criminal entangled in the mafia's web.

Finally, Sophia found herself in a secluded alley, her breath ragged and her body trembling with exhaustion. The adrenaline began to ebb, leaving a sense of vulnerability in its wake. She leaned against a cold brick wall, tears streaming down her cheeks as the weight of her choices crashed down upon her.

As the night enveloped her, Sophia made a silent vow—a vow to uncover the truth, to find a way to redeem herself and those she cared about. She yearned for a life where love, justice, and her own identity could coexist harmoniously.

Chapter 2 ended with Sophia standing in that desolate alley, her resolve strengthened amidst the chaos and uncertainty that lay ahead. The twists of fate had thrown her into a dangerous game, and she was determined to play her hand with clarity and purpose. Little did she know that the journey she had embarked upon was far from over, and the challenges she would face would test her in ways she never could have anticipated.

As the echoes of her footsteps faded into the night, Sophia took her first steps towards unraveling the intricacies of her entanglement with the mafia, the FBI, and the collision of her own desires and convictions. The path ahead promised peril, but also the possibility of redemption and a chance to reclaim the life she had nearly lost in the pursuit of power and adventure.

Chapter 3: The Tangled Web

Sophia stood at the crossroads of her tumultuous life, the echoes of her footsteps fading into the night. Determination coursed through her veins as she wiped away the tears that stained her cheeks. It was time to untangle the web she had woven, to confront the consequences of her choices and find a way to redeem herself.

With renewed resolve, Sophia set out on a relentless quest for the truth, her path illuminated by a flickering streetlamp that cast long shadows on the cobblestone streets. She delved into the depths of her past, unearthing forgotten memories and connections that held the key to unraveling the mysteries surrounding her entanglement with the mafia.

As she ventured further, Sophia discovered a labyrinth of deceit, betrayal, and hidden agendas that extended far beyond her initial involvement. The web of corruption reached into the highest echelons of power, entangling politicians, businessmen, and even members of law enforcement. The lines between friend and foe blurred, leaving her unsure of who she could trust.

Guided by her instincts and driven by a thirst for justice, Sophia sought out unlikely allies in the shadows. She reached out to contacts from her past, individuals with their own motivations and secrets, who could provide the missing pieces of the puzzle. Together, they formed a clandestine network of truth-seekers, united by their shared desire to expose the dark underbelly of the city and bring those responsible to justice.

As the investigation deepened, Sophia's paths crossed with Alex once again. He had been diligently working the case, unraveling threads of corruption from within the FBI itself. The shock of discovering Sophia's involvement with the mafia had ignited a fire within him, fueling his determination to uncover the truth and protect her from the dangerous forces at play.

Their reunion was fraught with tension and unspoken emotions. Sophia wrestled with guilt and the weight of her secrets, while Alex grappled with conflicting feelings of duty and his undeniable connection to her. Their shared mission drew them closer, forging a bond that transcended the boundaries of their respective roles.

Together, Sophia and Alex navigated the treacherous landscape of deception, piecing together fragments of information and following a trail of breadcrumbs that led them closer to the heart of the criminal empire. They confronted danger at every turn, narrowly escaping capture and eluding the relentless pursuit of those who sought to silence them.

As they delved deeper, the true extent of the mafia's operations came to light. Human trafficking, drug smuggling, and money laundering were just the tip of the iceberg. Sophia and Alex uncovered a web of interconnected criminal enterprises, each thread leading to the next in a complex dance of power and greed.

Their investigation took them to the darkest corners of the city, where the downtrodden and forgotten were trapped in a cycle of exploitation. Sophia's heart bled for the innocent victims caught in the crossfire, fueling her determination to dismantle the empire that perpetuated their suffering.

In a daring move, Sophia and Alex orchestrated a sting operation, their plan carefully crafted to expose the key players in the criminal organization. The operation teetered on a knife's edge, the slightest misstep threatening to unravel everything they had worked for. The tension reached its peak as they confronted the mastermind behind it all, the puppeteer who had manipulated lives and fortunes with impunity.

In a climactic showdown, Sophia faced her greatest test—confronting Anthony, the man who had both captivated and betrayed her. Their meeting was fraught with emotions, their histories and desires colliding in a maelstrom of conflicting loyalties. The truth unfurled, laying bare the depths of Anthony's deception and the price he had paid to maintain his position within the mafia.

In the end, Sophia made a choice that would forever change the course of her life. She refused to be defined by the darkness that had consumed her, choosing instead to embrace the light of truth and justice. With the evidence they had gathered, Sophia and Alex brought down the criminal empire, exposing the rot that had plagued the city for far too long.

Chapter 3 concluded with Sophia standing amidst the ruins of the empire she had helped dismantle, her heart heavy with the weight of the choices she had made. The path of redemption had come at great personal cost, but she had emerged stronger, her spirit unbreakable.

As the dust settled, Sophia and Alex stood side by side, their eyes fixed on the horizon. Their journey was far from over, as new challenges and dangers awaited them. But armed with the truth and a shared purpose, they were ready to face whatever lay ahead, knowing that their intertwined destinies had brought them together for a reason. Together, they would forge a future where justice prevailed and love conquered the darkest of shadows.

Chapter 4: Shadows of Redemption

The city breathed a sigh of relief as the criminal empire crumbled under the weight of Sophia and Alex's relentless pursuit of justice. The once-omnipotent figures who had reveled in their power now found themselves shackled by the chains of their own corruption. But the victory came at a price—a price both personal and profound.

In the aftermath of the takedown, Sophia and Alex faced the daunting task of rebuilding their lives. The scars left by their entanglement with the mafia ran deep, and the shadows of their past threatened to cast a pall over their future.

Sophia, haunted by the choices she had made, embarked on a journey of self-discovery. She sought solace in the quiet corners of the city, immersing herself in the arts and the stories of those who had triumphed over adversity. Through their tales of resilience and redemption, she found inspiration and the strength to confront her own demons.

With each passing day, Sophia shed the weight of guilt, allowing herself to believe in the possibility of forgiveness and a life beyond the darkness that had consumed her. She found comfort in her burgeoning relationship with Alex, their connection deepening as they navigated the complexities of their shared past. Together, they forged a bond built on trust, understanding, and a shared commitment to making amends.

But as they began to rebuild their lives, a new threat loomed on the horizon. The remnants of the dismantled criminal empire, like tendrils of smoke, sought to regroup and reclaim their lost power. Shadows moved in the periphery, whispers of vengeance echoing through the city's underbelly.

Sophia and Alex knew that their battle was far from over. They recognized the need to remain vigilant, to protect the fragile peace they had fought so hard to achieve. They gathered a small, dedicated team of allies— a mosaic of individuals with unique skills and shared determination. Together, they formed a clandestine force, an unseen shield against the encroaching darkness.

Their efforts took them on a perilous path, navigating treacherous alliances and unearthing hidden secrets that threatened to unravel the fragile stability they had fought to establish. The remnants of the criminal empire proved resilient, weaving a web of deception that tested Sophia and Alex's resolve at every turn.

As the stakes grew higher, they found themselves entangled in a conspiracy that reached far beyond the city limits. The corruption they had exposed was merely a symptom of a more insidious disease—a network of power that extended its tendrils into the highest echelons of society and government.

Amidst their crusade, Sophia and Alex discovered a pivotal figure—a puppet master orchestrating the chaos from the shadows. Layers of intrigue and manipulation unraveled, revealing a malevolent force that had eluded their grasp until now. With each revelation, they realized that their fight for justice had become a battle for the very soul of the city.

The lines between right and wrong blurred, as the true nature of the enemy they faced came into focus. The shadows of redemption cast doubt on their every move, challenging their resolve and the very foundations of their belief in justice. Sophia and Alex confronted their own limitations and vulnerabilities, forced to confront the darkness within themselves as they fought to overcome the darkness that threatened to consume the city.

In the final climactic showdown, Sophia and Alex faced the puppet master head-on. The battle tested their courage and determination, pushing them to the brink of their physical and emotional limits. Every decision carried weight, every step forward laced with uncertainty.

But in the end, it was their unwavering belief in the power of truth and justice that prevailed. The puppet master was unmasked, their manipulations laid bare for the world to see. The city exhaled a collective breath, its wounds beginning to heal as the grip of corruption loosened its hold.

Chapter 4 concluded with Sophia and Alex standing on the precipice of a new era—a city reborn from the ashes of its own darkness. The journey had been arduous, but they emerged stronger, their souls tempered by the trials they had faced.

As they looked out over the city they had fought so hard to save, a sense of hope blossomed within them. They knew that their work was far from finished, that the battle against corruption would be an ongoing struggle. But armed with the lessons they had learned and the bonds they had forged, they were ready to face whatever challenges lay ahead.

United in purpose and fueled by a shared vision of a brighter future, Sophia and Alex stepped forward, their shadows of redemption trailing behind them. The city awaited their leadership, their commitment to justice serving as a beacon of light in a world that had been shrouded in darkness for far too long.

Chapter 5: A New Dawn

The city breathed a collective sigh of relief as the grip of corruption finally loosened its hold. The remnants of the criminal empire had been dismantled, and the puppet master behind it all had been exposed. But as the dust settled, Sophia and Alex knew that their work was far from over. The city needed healing, and they were determined to lead the way.

Chapter 5 begins with Sophia and Alex standing at the precipice of a new dawn. The scars of their battles were visible, both physically and emotionally, but they wore them as badges of honor. They had emerged from the crucible of darkness stronger, more resilient, and ready to rebuild a city that had been battered by corruption.

Together, they formed a united front, a beacon of hope amidst the shadows of the past. Sophia's experiences had transformed her from a reluctant player in the criminal underworld to a warrior for justice. Her journey had taught her the true meaning of redemption, and she was determined to share that knowledge with others.

In the aftermath of their victories, Sophia and Alex reached out to the community, rallying the citizens to reclaim their city. They organized town hall meetings, where they listened to the concerns and grievances of the people. They sought to rebuild trust, to bridge the gap between the community and law enforcement, and to foster an environment of collaboration and unity.

With each step forward, Sophia and Alex encountered resistance from those who still clung to the remnants of the old regime. The shadows of corruption fought back, their tendrils stretching out in one last desperate attempt to regain control. But Sophia and Alex stood firm, unwavering in their commitment to the truth.

As they worked tirelessly to expose the remaining pockets of corruption, Sophia and Alex faced personal challenges as well. Their relationship, born out of shared adversity, was tested by the weight of their responsibilities. The scars of their past continued to haunt them, threatening to tear them apart. But they refused to let darkness prevail. Together, they found solace in each other, drawing strength from their love and shared purpose.

In the midst of their efforts, Sophia discovered a new passion—the power of education. She recognized that true change could only happen through the enlightenment of future generations. She spearheaded programs to empower underprivileged youth, offering them opportunities for education and mentorship. Through these initiatives, she aimed to break the cycle of poverty and vulnerability that had allowed corruption to thrive.

As the city began to heal, Sophia and Alex faced a formidable adversary—one who had remained hidden in the shadows, biding their time. This new threat posed a challenge unlike any they had faced before. They found themselves entangled in a web of political intrigue, where power and manipulation reigned supreme.

In their pursuit of justice, Sophia and Alex discovered that the roots of corruption ran deep, extending beyond the criminal underworld. They uncovered a network of influential figures whose actions perpetuated inequality and exploitation. The battle for the soul of the city had evolved into a fight against entrenched systems of oppression.

With the support of their dedicated team and the community, Sophia and Alex waged a war on multiple fronts. They exposed the corrupt politicians, businessmen, and other influential figures who had profited from the city's suffering. The truth became a weapon, shining a light on the darkest corners of society and forcing those in power to confront their own complicity.

In a dramatic climax, Sophia and Alex confronted the mastermind behind the web of political corruption. The battle tested their resolve, pushing them to their physical and emotional limits. They risked everything to expose the truth and ensure that justice prevailed.

As the final pieces fell into place, the city erupted in celebration. The once-entrenched systems of corruption were dismantled, and a wave of reform swept through the city. Sophia and Alex became symbols of hope, beacons of light in a world that had been shrouded in darkness for far too long.

Chapter 5 concludes with Sophia and Alex standing on the precipice of a new era. The city they had fought so hard to save was transformed—a place where justice reigned, where the voices of the marginalized were heard, and where the shadows of corruption were banished to the past.

They knew that their work was not yet complete. The fight against corruption would always be ongoing, and new challenges would arise. But armed with the lessons they had learned and the resilience they had forged, Sophia and Alex were prepared to face whatever obstacles lay ahead.

Together, they embraced the dawn of a new era—a city rebuilt from the ruins of its past. The journey had been arduous, but it had brought them to this defining moment. With hope in their hearts and the unwavering belief in the power of redemption, they stepped forward, ready to lead their city into a future where justice and compassion prevailed.

Chapter 6: The Resilience of Heroes

Chapter 6 begins with Sophia and Alex standing at the helm of a transformed city, basking in the glow of their hard-fought victories. The shadows of corruption had been banished, but the journey had taken its toll. They had faced unimaginable challenges, witnessed the depths of human depravity, and confronted their own inner demons. However, they knew that their work was not yet complete.

As the city recovered from the wounds inflicted by corruption, Sophia and Alex turned their attention to the process of healing. They recognized that the scars left by the dark days would take time to fade, and that true restoration required more than just dismantling criminal organizations. They embarked on a mission to rebuild not only the physical infrastructure but also the social fabric of the city.

Chapter 6 delves into the intricate process of rebuilding. Sophia and Alex worked tirelessly to establish programs that focused on rehabilitation and empowerment. They collaborated with community organizations, nonprofits, and government agencies to provide resources and support to those affected by the years of corruption.

One of their key initiatives was the creation of job training programs. They understood that unemployment and poverty were breeding grounds for crime, and that sustainable employment was essential for breaking the cycle. They partnered with local businesses to provide vocational training and job placement services, giving the people a chance to rebuild their lives with dignity and purpose.

Sophia, drawing on her own experiences, became a vocal advocate for mental health services. She recognized the lasting trauma inflicted upon the city's inhabitants and sought to provide them with the support they needed. She spearheaded the establishment of counseling centers and support groups, ensuring that no one would be left to suffer in silence.

In addition to physical and mental well-being, Sophia and Alex recognized the importance of fostering a sense of community and belonging. They organized neighborhood events, bringing people together to celebrate their resilience and forge connections. They also revitalized public spaces, transforming them into vibrant gathering places where people could come together, share stories, and find solace in one another's company.

But as the city began to heal, a new threat emerged—one that challenged the very foundations of their accomplishments. A wave of disillusionment swept through the city, as some questioned whether true change was possible or if corruption would simply find new ways to infiltrate their lives. Sophia and Alex were faced with the daunting task of restoring faith in the system and ensuring that the progress they had made was not in vain.

They launched a campaign to increase transparency and accountability in government. They pushed for reforms that would close loopholes and prevent the re-emergence of corruption. They encouraged citizen engagement, urging people to participate in the democratic process and hold their elected officials accountable. Sophia and Alex knew that the fight against corruption was not a one-time battle, but an ongoing effort that required constant vigilance.

Chapter 6 also explores the personal journeys of Sophia and Alex. The toll of their relentless pursuit of justice weighed heavily on their souls. They grappled with the question of whether the sacrifices they had made were worth it. They confronted their own vulnerabilities and insecurities, questioning whether they were truly deserving of the hero status bestowed upon them.

But in moments of doubt, they found strength in each other. Their love and unwavering support became a source of resilience, reminding them of the purpose that had driven them from the beginning. They realized that true heroes were not invincible, but ordinary individuals who chose to rise above their circumstances and fight for a better world.

In the midst of their personal struggles, Sophia and Alex discovered a new generation of heroes emerging from the shadows. Inspired by their example, individuals stepped forward to continue the work of rebuilding and reform. They recognized that change was a collective effort and that the resilience of heroes extended far beyond the actions of a few.

Chapter 6 concludes with Sophia and Alex standing on the precipice of a new chapter in their lives. The city they had fought so hard to save was on a path to recovery, but the journey was far from over. They knew that the battle against corruption would always be an ongoing struggle, requiring the commitment and dedication of generations to come.

With hope in their hearts and the knowledge that the resilience of heroes could overcome even the darkest of shadows, Sophia and Alex stepped forward, ready to face whatever challenges lay ahead. They embraced their role as catalysts for change, leading by example and inspiring others to join the fight.

The city, once shrouded in darkness, now stood as a beacon of hope—a testament to the indomitable spirit of its inhabitants. It was a reminder that even in the face of adversity, redemption was possible, and that the power to transform lay within the hearts of those who dared to dream of a better world.

www.ingramcontent.com/pod-product-compliance
Lightning Source LLC
Chambersburg PA
CBHW072055230526
45479CB00010B/1094